Everything has beauty, but not everyone sees it.
Confucius

In waking a tiger, use a long stick.
Mao Zedong

You have to believe in yourself.
Sun Tzu

The ladder of success is best climbed by stepping on the rungs of opportunity.

Ayn Rand

Without change, something sleeps inside us, and seldom awakens. The sleeper must awaken.

Frank Herbert

I am determined to be cheerful and happy in whatever situation I may find myself. For I have learned that the greater part of our misery or unhappiness is determined not by our circumstance but by our disposition.

Martha Washington

We gain strength, and courage, and confidence by each experience in which we really stop to look fear in the face... we must do that which we think we cannot.
Eleanor Roosevelt

That which does not kill us makes us stronger.
Friedrich Nietzsche

Character cannot be developed in ease and quiet. Only through experience of trial and suffering can the soul be strengthened, ambition inspired, and success achieved.
Helen Keller

Only one who devotes himself to a cause with his whole strength and soul can be a true master. For this reason mastery demands all of a person.

Albert Einstein

In matters of style, swim with the current; in matters of principle, stand like a rock.
Thomas Jefferson

The best and most beautiful things in the world cannot be seen or even touched - they must be felt with the heart.

Helen Keller

Health is the greatest gift, contentment the greatest wealth, faithfulness the best relationship.

Buddha

Happiness resides not in possessions, and not in gold, happiness dwells in the soul.

Democritus

Thousands of candles can be lighted from a single candle, and the life of the candle will not be shortened. Happiness never decreases by being shared.
Buddha

Believe you can and you're halfway there.
Theodore Roosevelt

You must do the things you think you cannot do.
Eleanor Roosevelt

Supreme excellence consists in breaking the enemy's resistance without fighting.
Sun Tzu

Being deeply loved by someone gives you strength, while loving someone deeply gives you courage.

Lao Tzu

you would be loved, love, and be loveable.
Benjamin Franklin

If you wished to be loved, love.
Lucius Annaeus Seneca

Human beings must be known to be loved; but Divine beings must be loved to be known.

Blaise Pascal

I know that I am intelligent, because I know that I know nothing.

Socrates

What we achieve inwardly will change outer reality.

Plutarch

Believe you can and you're halfway there.
Theodore Roosevelt

In a gentle way, you can shake the world.
Mahatma Gandhi

With self-discipline most anything is possible.
Theodore Roosevelt

A place for everything, everything in its place.
Benjamin Franklin

If we did all the things we are capable of, we would literally astound ourselves.

Thomas A. Edison

Look within. Within is the fountain of good, and it will ever bubble up, if thou wilt ever dig.
Marcus Aurelius

Be kind whenever possible. It is always possible.
Dalai Lama

Our greatest weakness lies in giving up. The most certain way to succeed is always to try just one more time.

Thomas A. Edison

A creative man is motivated by the desire to achieve, not by the desire to beat others.
Ayn Rand

With the new day comes new strength and new thoughts.
Eleanor Roosevelt

Optimism is the faith that leads to achievement. Nothing can be done without hope and confidence.
Helen Keller

You have to learn the rules of the game. And then you have to play better than anyone else.
Albert Einstein

The key is to keep company only with people who uplift you, whose presence calls forth your best.

Epictetus

By failing to prepare, you are preparing to fail.
Benjamin Franklin

Who seeks shall find.

Sophocles

Determine never to be idle. No person will have occasion to complain of the want of time who never loses any. It is wonderful how much may be done if we are always doing.

Thomas Jefferson

The more man meditates upon good thoughts, the better will be his world and the world at large.

Confucius

Quality is not an act, it is a habit.
Aristotle

Moral excellence comes about as a result of habit. We become just by doing just acts, temperate by doing temperate acts, brave by doing brave acts.

Aristotle

www.ingramcontent.com/pod-product-compliance
Lightning Source LLC
Chambersburg PA
CBHW041524280526

45792CB00004B/1373